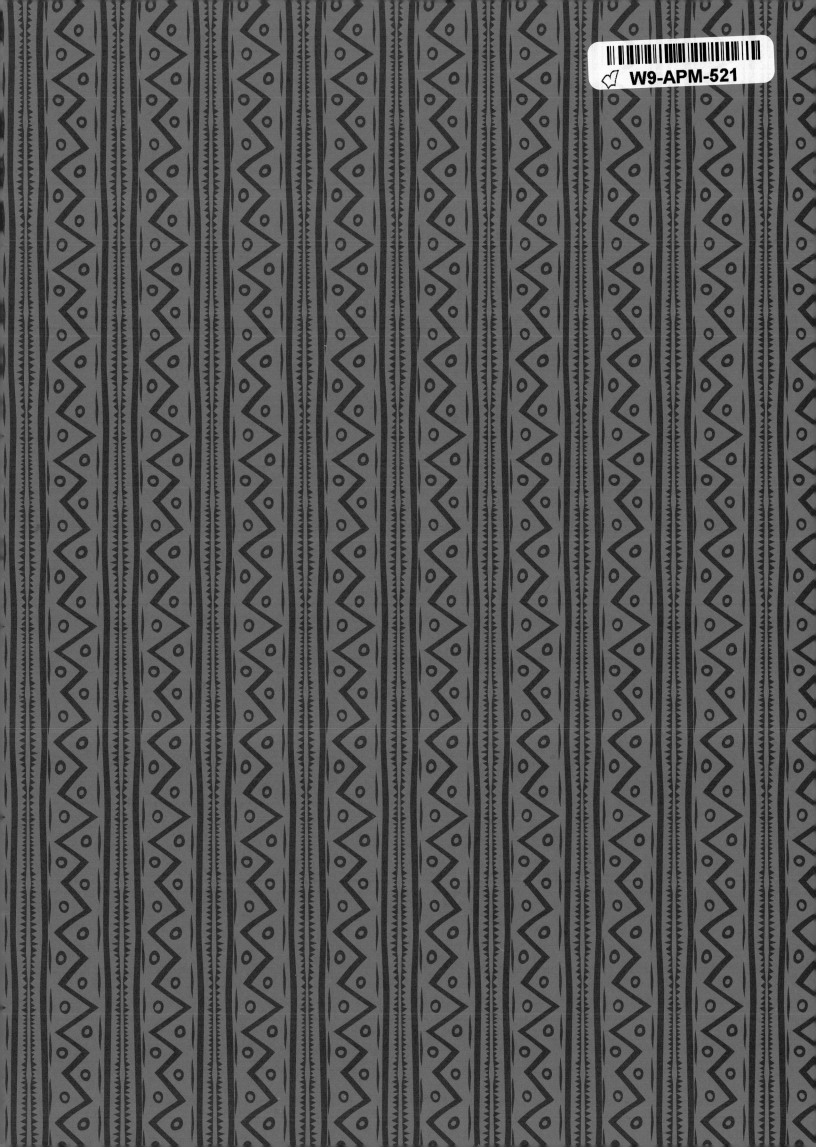

SWEET WORDS SO BRAVE

The Story
of
African American Literature

Written by Barbara K. Curry and James Michael Brodie
Illustrated by Jerry Butler

Zino Press

CHILDREN'S BOOKS

Madison, Wisconsin

The title *Sweet Words So Brave* is taken from the poem "Sweet Words on Race,"
published in *The Panther and the Lash,*
by Langston Hughes

Sweet Words So Brave: The Story of African American Literature is published by Zino Press Children's Books, PO Box 52, Madison, Wisconsin, 53701. Text copyright © 1996 by Barbara K. Curry and James Michael Brodie. Illustrations copyright © 1996 by Zino Press Children's Books. Entire contents copyright © 1996 by Zino Press Children's Books. All rights reserved. No parts of this book may be reproduced in any way, except for brief excerpts for review purposes in newspapers and magazines, without the express written permission of Zino Press Children's Books. Printed in U.S.A.

"I, Too" from *Selected Poems* by Langston Hughes. Copyright © 1926 by Alfred A. Knopf, Inc., and renewed 1954 by Langston Hughes. Reprinted by permission of the publisher. "We Real Cool" copyright © 1960 by Gwendolyn Brooks. Reprinted with permission of Gwendolyn Brooks. Excerpt from "Nikki-Rosa," from *Black Feeling, Black Talk/Black Judgement* by Nikki Giovanni, copyright © 1968, 1970 by Nikki Giovanni. Reprinted by permission of William Morrow & Co., Inc. Excerpt from *I Know Why the Caged Bird Sings* copyright © 1970 by Maya Angelou. Reprinted with permission of Random House, Inc.

Photos: Corbis-Bettmann, pages 15, 25, 27, 34, 35, 37, 38, 44, 45, 46, 47, 52, 53; Museum of the Confederacy, page 17; the Schomburg Center for the Study of Black Culture, page 26; UPI-Bettmann, pages 36, 44; Knowledge Unlimited archives, pages 10, 11, 12, 16, 24, 32, 33, 46.

Written by Barbara K. Curry and James Michael Brodie. Illustrated and designed by Jerry Butler. Edited by Dave Schreiner and Liza DiPrima. Art direction by Pat Ready. Educational consultant, April Hoffman.

Library of Congress Cataloging-in-Publication Data

Curry, Barbara K.
    Sweet words so brave : the story of African American literature / written by Barbara K. Curry and James Michael Brodie ; illustrated by Jerry Butler.
        p.   cm.
    Includes bibliographical references (p. 64)
    Summary: A survey of the history of African American literature, from slave narratives to the present, told in the voice of a grandfather speaking to his granddaughter.
    ISBN 1-55933-179-8 (hardcover : lib. bdg.)
    1. American literature—Afro-American authors—History and criticism—juvenile literature.   2. Afro-Americans—Intellectual life—Juvenile literature.   3. Afro-Americans in literature—Juvenile literature. [1. American literature—Afro-American authors—History and criticism.] I. Brodie, James Michael, 1957- . II. Butler, Jerry, 1947- ill.   III. Title.
PS153.N5C87   1996   96-18995
810.9'896073—dc20   CIP
                                                                                        AC

10 9 8 7 6 5 4 3 2 1
First Printing, December 1996

For our mothers — Carolyn Curry and Alberta Brodie
— BKC and JMB

I would like to dedicate this book to my daughters, Vanessa Rae Butler and Rachelle Leigh Butler, in recognition of the many hours of work and support they freely gave during the creation of the illustrations pictured here.
— JB

Please tell me a story. Write it down so I can put it in my pocket and carry it around. Tell me about the people from Africa who came before me. Tell me how they worked the fields, built this country and made it great. Tell me how the Africans fought to be free here. Tell me my history — but write it down so I can carry it with me.

Please tell me a story and make it sing for me. Draw word pictures of lovely blue skies, mist-green seas, and orchids growing wild on the sides of trees. Make me hear robins singing above me, bees buzzing close to my ear, crickets chirping in the fall of the year.

Tell me a story of foreign intrigue — about spies, secret places, dark passages, ancient lands.

Tell me a story so I can find myself. I'll be the warrior, the artist, the doctor, the chemist, the writer. The one who saves the world. I'll be on the pages doing my best for my country, for goodness, for the pursuit of happiness. Tell me a story. Tell me about me — but write it down so I can put it in my pocket and carry it around.

Come sit by me, child, I have stories to tell about folks from places like Nigeria and Senegal. They were orators turned into writers, brave all in all. I'll weave tales for you that stretch from past to present. Along the way we will meet people who struggled to be free, and we will rest for a while in a magical place called Harlem. Come with me. I've got stories to tell you. I've written them down — if you like them well enough, you can carry them with you all around town.

For Arabella

CHAPTER ONE

TO READ

TO WRITE

O BE FREE

Once there were folks brought to America from Africa to work in the fields. They came in chains, and once they got here they were whipped and beaten and treated cruelly. It was as if they weren't human beings. They were the property of the people who owned the farms and plantations where they worked. These unlucky Africans were slaves. They were separated from their families. Though they came from many different countries, with different languages and religions and stories to tell, their owners treated them like one single group, and tried to take their stories away. But the slaves kept their stories alive, telling them out loud to each other, and handing them down from one generation to the next, like I'm doing with you.

Many of their stories were about "tricksters," folks or animals who got into trouble and used their wits to save themselves. Brer Rabbit was one of the most popular characters in these stories. He could outsmart enemies like Brer Fox even though they were bigger and stronger than he was. These trickster tales helped the slaves pass their stories along. And the truth is, the slaves saw themselves like Brer Rabbit. They were being hurt by people who were stronger and had more power than they did. They had to use their brains to survive, too.

These slaves were forbidden to read and write. If they were caught writing, or teaching others how, they got punished. It was a brave man, woman, or child who picked up a book in those days.

9

But people picked them up anyway. They stole away at night, after chores. Their classrooms were moonlit hiding places, their notebooks were made of slate. They used chalk stone to write. They remembered the stories from their lives in Africa. They held those stories firm in their hands like delicate glow flies. Their closed fists lit up the night and their voices carried lovely songs from deep in their throats over the night breeze. Those folks pooled their different traditions to make one. They created new lives — new songs, new customs, new stories — out of pieces of their old lives and pieces of the lives they had now. They were not free, but they were very brave.

One of them was Olaudah Equiano. You pronounce that oo-LAW-dah eh-kwee-AH-no. He was born in the village of Esseka, in what's now called Nigeria, in around 1745. His daddy was a tribal elder, and Olaudah was going to be a leader in his community.

But when he was 11, he and his sister were taken into slavery. They never saw each other again. They never saw their African home again. Even his name was taken away. He got a new "slave" name — Gustavus Vassa.

Olaudah was owned by many people — a Virginia farmer, a British Navy officer, and a Pennsylvania shop owner. Unlike most slaves, he was able to earn some money for his work, and when he was 20, he managed to buy his own freedom, which was something very few slaves could do. After he was freed, he went to live in England.

$150 REWARD

RANAWAY from the subscriber, on the night of the 2d instant, a negro man, who calls himself *Henry May*, about 22 years old, 5 feet 6 or 8 inches high, ordinary color, rather chunky built, bushy head, and has it divided mostly on one side, and keeps it very nicely combed; has been raised in the house, and is a first rate dining-room servant, and was in a tavern in Louisville for 18 months. I expect he is now in Louisville trying to make his escape to a free state, (in all probability to Cincinnati, Ohio.) Perhaps he may try to get employment on a steamboat. He is a good cook, and is handy in any capacity as a house servant. Had on when he left, a dark cassinett coatee, and dark striped cassinett pantaloons, new—he had other clothing. I will give $50 reward if taken in Louisville; 100 dollars if taken one hundred miles from Louisville in this State, and 150 dollars if taken out of this State, and delivered to me, or secured in any jail so that I can get him again.

WILLIAM BURKE.

Bardstown, Ky., September 3d, 1838.

BY

HEWLETT & BRIGHT.

SALE OF

VALUABLE SLAVES,

(On account of departure)

The Owner of the following named and valuable Slaves, being on the eve of departure for Europe, will cause the same to be offered for sale, at the NEW EXCHANGE, corner of St. Louis and Chartres streets, on *Saturday,* May 16, at Twelve o'Clock, *viz.*

1. **SARAH,** a mulatress, aged 45 years, a good cook and accustomed to house work in general, is an excellent and faithful nurse for sick persons, and in every respect a first rate character.

2. **DENNIS,** her son, a mulatto, aged 24 years, a first rate cook and steward for a vessel, having been in that capacity for many years on board one of the Mobile packets; is strictly honest, temperate, and a first rate subject.

3. **CHOLE,** a mulatress, aged 36 years, she is, without exception, one of the most competent servants in the country, a first rate washer and ironer, does up lace, a good cook, and for a bachelor who wishes a house-keeper she would be invaluable: she is also a good ladies' maid, having travelled to the North in that capacity.

4. **FANNY,** her daughter, a mulatress, aged 16 years, speaks French and English, is a superior hair-dresser, (pupil of Guilliac,) a good seamstress and ladies' maid, is smart, intelligent, and a first rate character.

5. **DANDRIDGE,** a mulatoo, aged 26 years, a first rate dining-room servant, a good painter and rough carpenter, and has but few equals for honesty and sobriety.

6. **NANCY,** his wife, aged about 24 years, a confidential house servant, good seamstress, mantuamaker and tailoress, a good cook, washer and ironer, etc.

7. **MARY ANN,** her child, a creole, aged 7 years, speaks French and English, is smart, active and intelligent.

8. **FANNY or FRANCES,** a mulatress, aged 22 years, is a first rate washer and ironer, good cook and house servant, and has an excellent character.

9. **EMMA,** an orphan, aged 10 or 11 years, speaks French and English, has been in the country 7 years, has been accustomed to waiting on table, sewing etc.; is intelligent and active.

10. **FRANK,** a mulatto, aged about 32 years speaks French and English, is a first rate hostler and coachman, understands perfectly well the management of horses, and is, in every respect, a first rate character, with the exception that he will occasionally drink, though not an habitual drunkard.

☞ All the above named Slaves are acclimated and excellent subjects; they were purchased by their present vendor many years ago, and will, therefore, be severally warranted against all vices and maladies prescribed by law, save and except FRANK, who is fully guaranteed in every other respect but the one above mentioned.

TERMS:—One-half Cash, and the other half in notes at Six months, drawn and endorsed to the satisfaction of the Vendor, with special mortgage on the Slaves until final payment. The Acts of Sale to be passed before WILLIAM BOSWELL, *Notary Public,* at the expense of the Purchaser.

New-Orleans, May 13, 1835.

Olaudah wrote a book about his life, *The Interesting Narrative of the Life of Olaudah Equiano, or Gustavus Vassa, the African, Written by Himself.* This is one of the first written stories by a slave about his own life. It's called a "slave narrative." People who read this book learned about the horrors of slavery. Olaudah spent the rest of his life fighting to end the slave trade.

Phillis Wheatley was another early writer. She was born in about 1753 in what's now Senegal. Phillis came to America in chains when she was about eight years old. She was given her name by John Wheatley, a Boston merchant. The Wheatleys were different from most slave owners. Using the Bible, they helped Phillis learn to read and write.

Phillis wrote poems. She was sickly much of her life, and she used her

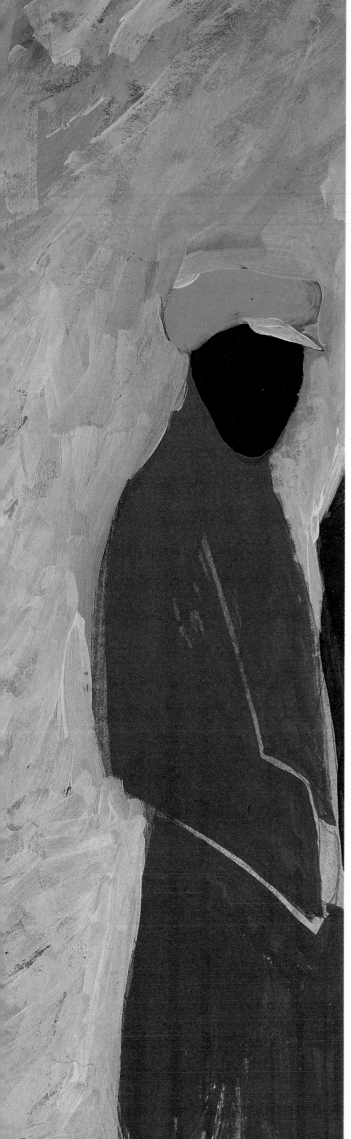

poetry to go places her fragile body couldn't take her. Her first poem was printed in 1767. In 1773, she traveled to London, England. That same year, her first book of poems was printed there. It's the first book of poetry ever published by an African American. Phillis's poems are old-fashioned

Phillis Wheatley

sounding. She wrote about religion and her life in America and England. And she wrote some about her life as a slave.

Phillis got her freedom in 1773, and a few years later, she married John Peters, a free black man. They had three children. Sorry to say, all of them died as babies, and Phillis herself died when she was only 31 years old. Phillis and Olaudah proved to whites that black people could read, and they could write with their minds and hearts.

Well look here, child, come on. We can't stay here much longer. I have more stories to tell. Before we go, you've got to meet William Wells Brown and Frederick Douglass. They also wrote during the time of slavery. Their writings helped free the slaves.

William Wells Brown was a high-spirited and brave man. He wrote a book that folks are still fighting about. It's called *Clotel: Or, the President's Daughter*. It was a made-up story, called a novel, about a woman who some folks think was the daughter of a slave named Sally Hemmings and Thomas Jefferson. That book got a lot of people talking. People got pretty upset with William about it, but he didn't care. *Clotel* is the first novel written by an African American.

William was born around 1814 near Lexington, Kentucky. His mother was a slave. As a boy, he was "hired out" — allowed to work other jobs for different slave owners and other folks. When he was about 20 years old, William ran away to the North. On the way, he met a Quaker named Wells Brown. Quakers didn't believe in slavery, and Mr. Brown helped William escape. The story goes that William was so grateful for Mr. Brown's help that he changed his own name to William Wells Brown.

William didn't just write that one book. He also wrote about his life as a slave and he wrote anti-slavery songs. He traveled all over America and Europe speaking out against slavery.

Frederick Douglass was one of the most powerful and important writers of the 19th century. His full name was Frederick Augustus Washington Bailey. He changed it to Frederick Douglass later on. He was born a slave around 1817. In 1838, he ran away and spent his life fighting against slavery. He wrote a book about his life, *Narrative of the Life of Frederick Douglass, an American Slave, Written by Himself*. That book is probably the most famous slave narrative of them all.

Frederick was taken from his mama as a baby and raised on a Maryland

Frederick Douglass

plantation. When he was about eight years old, he was sent to Baltimore to the home of Hugh Auld. There, Frederick got his first taste of learning. And that was all he needed. Mrs. Auld taught him his ABC's, and Frederick took it from there.

He realized that reading and writing would give him power. He figured it would be much harder for people to keep him a slave if he had that power. He was right.

Frederick learned to read and write any way he could. He got poor white boys to teach him by giving them bread from the Aulds' kitchen. And he sometimes tricked white boys into helping him by telling them he could write better than they could. In the beginning, he didn't know many letters, but he learned the words they wrote. Pretty soon, he didn't need their "help" anymore.

Frederick was sent to another plantation when he was 15. He ran away six years later and went north, where he became famous as a powerful speaker against slavery. Many people listened to what he had to say. They took him seriously because he had been a slave himself. After his book was published in 1845, Frederick went to England, where he spoke against slavery. When he came back he had enough money to buy his own freedom. Then he started a newspaper called the North Star that called for the abolition, or getting rid, of slavery. Frederick Douglass was an important man. His tireless work helped end slavery in this country.

In 1861, a war called the Civil War started. It was fought between the northern part of the United States, which didn't have slavery, and the South, which did. At the end of the Civil War, slavery was ended and black people were free. For a time, they could vote, and some were even elected to Congress in the South. But then the rights they won got taken away from them. First came the Ku Klux Klan. This started out as a group of white men who had fought for the South in the Civil War. They rode around in hoods, frightening black people and sometimes killing them. Then came "Jim Crow" laws. These laws separated white and black people. They made it almost impossible for blacks to vote in many places. They took jobs away from blacks, and kept them from eating in restaurants, going to schools, or even drinking from fountains that whites could use. Then in 1896, the Supreme Court, the highest court in the country, said it was all right to keep black and white children in separate schools. That made Jim Crow the law of the land.

Black people faced another great danger. In the South, blacks got lynched, or killed, by angry mobs of white people. Many times, members of the Klan were behind these killings. But black people kept on fighting, any way they could. One of the people who fought hardest was Ida Wells Barnett. Ida was a teacher and the editor of a newspaper in Memphis, Tennessee. In 1892, she printed the names of some people who had lynched three black men. You can bet she was brave for doing that. A mob of whites wrecked her newspaper offices, so Ida moved north to New York and then to Chicago. She kept right on working to stop lynchings.

Many other black people kept on writing, although it wasn't easy for them. Most of them didn't get the

At left: Africans were jammed into ships for the journey to America, called the "Middle Passage."
Below: A group of slaves in Virginia in the early 1860s

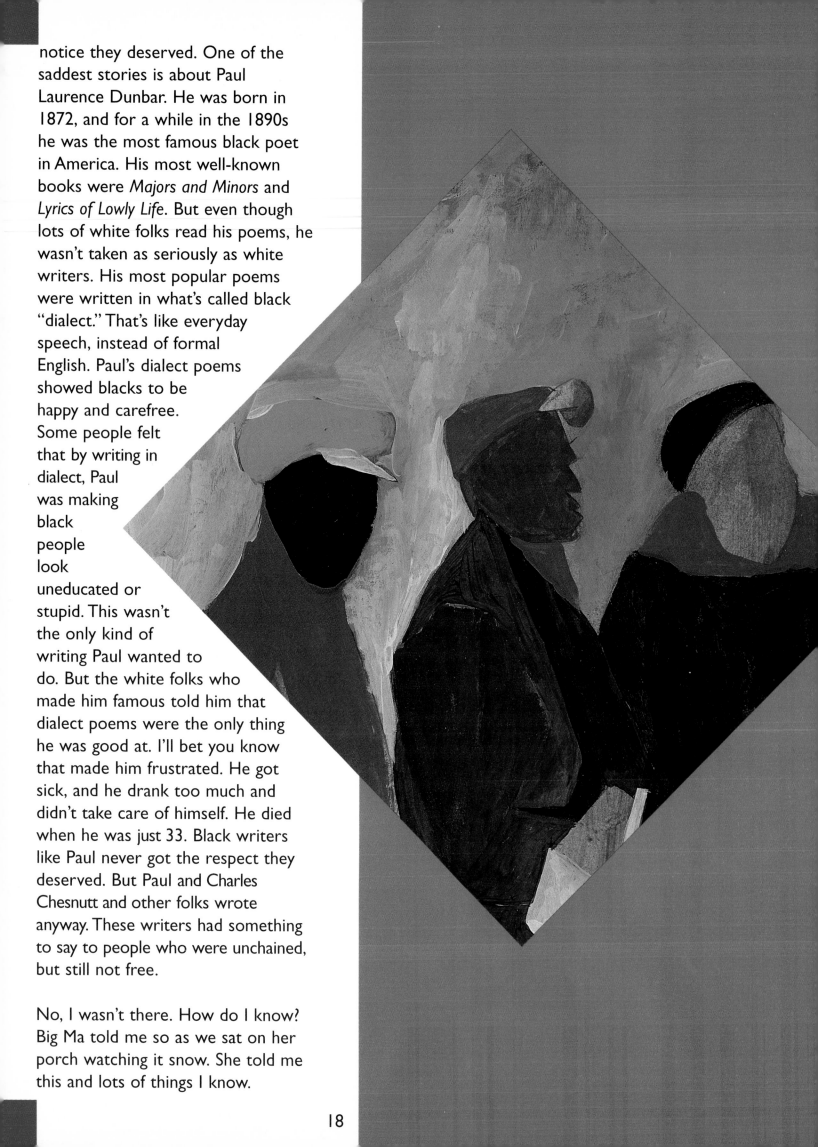

notice they deserved. One of the saddest stories is about Paul Laurence Dunbar. He was born in 1872, and for a while in the 1890s he was the most famous black poet in America. His most well-known books were *Majors and Minors* and *Lyrics of Lowly Life*. But even though lots of white folks read his poems, he wasn't taken as seriously as white writers. His most popular poems were written in what's called black "dialect." That's like everyday speech, instead of formal English. Paul's dialect poems showed blacks to be happy and carefree. Some people felt that by writing in dialect, Paul was making black people look uneducated or stupid. This wasn't the only kind of writing Paul wanted to do. But the white folks who made him famous told him that dialect poems were the only thing he was good at. I'll bet you know that made him frustrated. He got sick, and he drank too much and didn't take care of himself. He died when he was just 33. Black writers like Paul never got the respect they deserved. But Paul and Charles Chesnutt and other folks wrote anyway. These writers had something to say to people who were unchained, but still not free.

No, I wasn't there. How do I know? Big Ma told me so as we sat on her porch watching it snow. She told me this and lots of things I know.

Frederick Douglass:

Very soon after I went to live with Mr. and Mrs. Auld, she very kindly commenced to teach me the A, B, C. After I had learned this, she assisted me in learning to spell words of three or four letters. Just at this point of my progress, Mr. Auld found out what was going on, and at once forbade Mrs. Auld to instruct me further, telling her, among other things, that it was unlawful, as well as unsafe, to teach a slave to read. ... The very decided manner with which he spoke, and strove to impress his wife with the evil consequences of giving me instruction, served to convince me that he was deeply sensible of the truths he was uttering. ... What he most dreaded, that I most desired. ... [A]nd the argument which he so warmly urged, against my learning to read, only served to inspire me with a desire and determination to learn.

from *Narrative of the Life of Frederick Douglass, an American Slave, Written by Himself*

CHAPTER TWO

"We"—A People

Lift every voice and sing

Till earth and heaven ring,

Ring with the harmonies of Liberty;

Let our rejoicing rise

High as the listening skies, ...

Let us march on till victory is won.

"ift Every Voice and Sing" — James Weldon Johnson wrote that. People have called it "the Negro National Anthem." James wrote a lot of other things, too. One of them was a novel called *The Autobiography of an Ex-Colored Man.* This famous book was about a black man who pretends to be white. It got people thinking about what it means to be black or white in America. James was one of the people working during the Harlem Renaissance, a very special time for writing, music, and art.

Have you heard of Harlem, youngster? Great things happened there. Come hear my words, I will soothe you with a song and comfort you with a blanket of stories. Come relax in the magic of the Harlem Renaissance.

Clockwise from the left: Composer and musician Duke Ellington; the Duke Ellington Orchestra in the 1920s; Langston Hughes; Harlem's famed Cotton Club in the 1930s; Mamie Smith, the first African American known to have made a recording

At the end of World War One, black folks moved north to places like Baltimore, Philadelphia, Chicago, and New York looking for chances to live the good life. The "good life," youngster, is the American dream. My daddy used to say it was "a job, a roof over your head, three meals a day, and a little money in the bank — or stuffed in a mattress for a rainy day." That was the dream of most folks.

The symbol of African American dreams was Harlem in New York City, where writers, musicians, and artists got together to talk about their lives and history. There was lots going on in Harlem. Folks were singing the blues, playing jazz, dancing, and those who couldn't do that were listening and tappin' their toes.

People were acting out stories in grand theaters. And writers caught people's imaginations with poetry, stories, and novels. African Americans were writing about their own lives, not as slaves or in political speeches, but as people. They were using language and music and rhythms in new and beautiful ways.

Langston Hughes was *the* man of the Harlem Renaissance. James Mercer Langston Hughes. He took the sounds of folks praying, singing, dancing, laughing, and crying, and the sounds of blues and jazz and all the music of Harlem, and added his own words. He was a poet and the soul of Harlem, and one of the most important writers of this century, white or black.

Langston was born in Joplin, Missouri, in 1902. He and his mama were poor. He went from place to place, and he was raised by his grandmama for a while.

Langston was always interested in writing, and when he was 19, his poetry was printed for the first time in a magazine called *The Crisis*. It was the magazine of the NAACP — the National Association for the Advancement of Colored People. A great man named W.E.B. Du Bois helped start the NAACP, and was the editor of *The Crisis* for a long time. Langston studied at Columbia University in New York City, but he left after a year. He took a job as a cabin boy on a merchant freighter and traveled to West Africa and to Europe. But eventually, he ended up in Harlem.

Langston went back to school and studied at Lincoln University, in

Pennsylvania. He started a magazine called *Fire!* at Lincoln with another writer named Zora Neale Hurston and other folks. Langston traveled around all his life, but he always returned to Harlem.

Everybody knew Langston. In 1926, his first book, *The Weary Blues*, was published. His poetry described life in Harlem — the dancers at the Cotton Club and the singers at the Apollo Theater, and also the troubles of just getting by. You can catch the rhythm of the music that was pouring out all over Harlem just from the sound of Langston's words. That rhythm showed up in his plays and operas. Langston also wrote stories about a man named Jesse B. Semple, or Simple for short, who wasn't too smart about some things, but who knew a lot about life.

Speaking of Zora Neale Hurston, she was a proud black woman, born in 1891. She was raised in the all-black town of Eatonville, Florida. Growing up there, Zora didn't feel a lot of the prejudice that other black people felt. Years later, some people said that Zora never spoke out enough for the Civil Rights Movement. But Zora said she never felt the need — she always felt like she was equal to whites.

Zora had to work hard to get herself an education. She moved around a lot and worked as a maid. But finally, she went to New York to study at Barnard College and Columbia University.

During the Harlem Renaissance, people got interested in the old-time stories, or folktales, of black people. They paid Zora to find these stories.

Zora Neale Hurston

These folktales had been passed down for a long time, but it took Zora to write them down. She went to the South and even to Haiti looking for these stories.

But Zora's most famous book is *Their Eyes Were Watching God*, a story about a woman named Janie who has a lot of adventures and troubles as she learns how to be her own person. *Their Eyes Were Watching God* shows off Zora's writing style: soft, poetic, almost like music. Youngster, you haven't lived 'til you've read this book.

Zora's last novel was printed in 1948. By that time, she'd started to get folks angry with some of her opinions, and people weren't so interested in what she had to say. Two years later, she left New York for good and went home to Florida. After she died in 1960, people forgot about her for a while, until new writers like Alice Walker discovered her again and woke people up to how great she was.

W.E.B. Du Bois

These writers and a lot of others, like Jean Toomer, Claude McKay, and Countee Cullen, wrote about life and kept folks informed during the Harlem Renaissance. People read the *Amsterdam News, Opportunity* magazine, and *The Crisis*.

What did all this reading mean? It meant that folks felt free to explore new ideas and experiment with new ways of writing and thinking.

Many writers used jazz rhythms in their work, the way Langston did. Or they wrote in black dialect, the way Paul Laurence Dunbar had.

Even though folks were writing and talking all the time, black people still struggled against a lot of prejudice and hate. Things hadn't changed much, and blacks still didn't get the same chances, or the same respect, that whites did. But lots of people were working to change that. Folks fell asleep with books under their pillows, and ideas about unity and black nationalism working in their heads. These folks felt that if they couldn't be at home in America, maybe they should go someplace else to live. Maybe even back to Africa — which a man named Marcus Garvey wanted them to do. A lot of writers moved between the United States and Europe, saying what was on their minds, itching, scratching, and searching for more freedom.

Richard Wright

27

Richard Wright was one of them. He wasn't really part of the Harlem Renaissance, because he did his writing after it was over. But he knew Langston Hughes and other folks who were part of the Renaissance.

Richard was born around Natchez, Mississippi, in 1908. He was a poor child like a lot of folks. Yes, indeed — there were times when he went to bed hungry. Richard, his mama, and his brother moved around a lot. They lived with his grandmama and with other relatives. Richard's mama even had to put him and his brother into an orphanage for a little while so they'd get fed regularly.

Even though Richard didn't get much formal schooling, he read everything he could get his hands on. When he was 17, he moved to Memphis, Tennessee. Now in Memphis at that time, it was against the law for a black person to check a book out of the library. But Richard didn't let that stop him. He borrowed a library card from a white man, then forged a note to the librarian: "Dear Madam: Will you please let this nigger boy have some books by H.L. Mencken?" Then he signed the white man's name. The librarian assumed the books were for the white man. She never suspected a thing.

With all that moving around, it's no wonder Richard got what folks used to call "wandering urges." It was hard for him to stay long in a place; he wanted to roam the country and see other places. Some folks are like that. Richard moved from Mississippi to Memphis to Chicago. The whole time, he was looking for a place where black people were treated equal to whites. He joined the Communist Party for a little while, because he thought they might be more fair to black folks. He left when he decided they weren't. Eventually, Richard ended up in New York, where he met Langston Hughes. Good old Langston again!

Being poor seemed to inspire Richard. He wrote a book called *Uncle Tom's Children* about life in the Jim Crow South. And then he wrote a big book called *Native Son. Native Son* is about a poor man named Bigger Thomas who accidentally kills his white boss's daughter. That book upset a lot of people, because it didn't come out happy at the end, and there were no good guys. But that's the way Richard wanted it. He thought that if people spent too much time feeling sorry for his characters, they wouldn't pay attention to what he had to say. *Native Son* was the first book by an African American to be read by a big audience of both blacks and whites.

Richard moved to Paris, France, in 1947. He stayed there for the rest of his life. But even when he moved to Paris, he kept on writing about the problems that black people have in America. There are people who say Richard was the best of all of the writers of his day. That's a large claim, youngster. And it just might be true.

Meanwhile, things were changing in America. More and more African Americans were moving to the North, looking for a better life. And when World War Two came along, the country went through a big change.

Langston Hughes:

I, TOO

I, too, sing America

I am the darker brother.
They send me to eat in the kitchen
When company comes,
But I laugh,
And eat well,
And grow strong.

Tomorrow,
I'll be at the table
When company comes.
Nobody'll dare
Say to me,
"Eat in the kitchen,"
Then.

Besides,
They'll see how beautiful I am
And be ashamed —

I, too, am America.

You're in the Army now. You're not behind a plow. You'll never get rich by digging a ditch. You're in the Army now."

I remember that song, youngster. Those were the days. The Second World War was over, but a bunch of us boys who served would find each other in the old neighborhood. To impress the girls we would "high step" and practice drills in the middle of the street. I caught the twinkle in one of those girls' eyes during those "showing off" times. I proposed to her. She is your grandmama, youngster.

Yeah, we stepped and marched and ran drill teams with folks in the neighborhood who wanted to be fancy.

It seemed like Harlem's magic wore off there for a while. The Great Depression hit us all pretty hard. That was a bad time, when many people in this country lost their jobs. Lots of folks didn't know where their next meal was coming from. The whole country was poor, but black folks were the poorest of all. When it came to jobs, black people were the "last ones hired and the first ones fired." And there weren't many jobs. Then World War Two began. Some black leaders like A. Philip Randolph visited the president of the United States and told him that they would march on Washington if something wasn't done about hiring blacks. President Franklin Roosevelt agreed it wasn't fair that black people were kept out of jobs back home while they were fighting for their country

TO BE

REE ONCE MORE

overseas. He ordered all the defense factories — the places making planes, tanks, and other military equipment — not to discriminate against black people when hiring. That meant black people couldn't be kept out of jobs just because of their color.

Then there was the war itself. Did I ever tell you about the Tuskegee Airmen? Those boys flew planes as if they were born with wings. They flew in a unit with just African American airmen. That wasn't surprising. All us black soldiers and airmen fought in our own units. It wasn't until the war was over that the government ordered the military to include black men in all the units.

At the end of the war, we all came home to get our lives in order again. Jim Crow laws still segregated folks along color lines. We black folks lived in our own world — our own neighborhoods and communities —

but the times were changing. The war did part of that. For one thing, a man named Jackie Robinson broke the "color line" in major league baseball. He became the first black player in the big leagues. He played for a team called the Brooklyn Dodgers. There were plenty of other good players before him, but they were only allowed to play against each other in the Negro Leagues. But with Jackie the thinking was, if blacks fought for America in a war, they should be able to play baseball for any team. Jackie had a tough time at first, but he played so well he won the hearts of his teammates, then Brooklyn, and then the whole country. Soon there were a lot more black ballplayers.

Jackie Robinson, the first black major league ballplayer in the 20th century

A. Philip Randolph, a civil rights and union leader

When the war ended, even more people moved to the big cities, and that made for some changes in how people lived. People were driving cars, watching television, talking to each other more and more on the telephone. You probably think those things have been around forever, youngster, but a lot of people were only beginning to buy and use them.

After the war, those writers who had slowed down got going again. They wrote about fairness, justice, and responsibility. They inspired children and grownups alike. They asked questions about life and the right of people to take part in their government, to be free, to question, to change, to have a better future for themselves and their children.

One of them was named Ralph Waldo Ellison. Ralph was born in Oklahoma City in 1914. His daddy named him after the writer Ralph Waldo Emerson.

Ralph knew his daddy from stories his mama told him. Ralph's daddy was a construction worker. He wanted Ralph to grow up and be a great poet.

He died when Ralph was three. His mom raised him and his brother alone after that. Ralph's mama was a woman who believed in freedom. She led protests against segregation and, even though she didn't have much money, she raised her sons with college in mind. Mrs. Ellison worked as a maid in the homes of rich white folks. Lots of times, she would bring home old magazines, books, and opera records that were being thrown away. You can bet Ralph gobbled those things up!

Ralph wanted to be a sculptor, and he also thought about being a musician or a composer. As it turned out, he got to be friends with Richard Wright. It was Richard who convinced Ralph to be a writer. After serving in the Merchant Marine during World War Two, Ralph came back to Harlem. There he wrote a book that people call a classic. That means it's a great book, youngster. The book is called *Invisible Man,* and it's about a black man who has a lot of bad experiences just trying to live and make things better for himself and other black people. He learns that nobody sees him as himself because they can't see beyond his skin color. He is "invisible" to others, but he finally finds out all about himself. People have said that *Invisible Man* is the best book written in America since World War Two. It doesn't have any easy answers. But that's why lots of people say it's so good.

The Ku Klux Klan remained strong in the 1940s and 1950s. Here a group of Klansmen march on Washington, D.C.

Ralph Ellison

Ralph went to the Tuskegee Institute in Alabama. He left after three years because of a mix-up in his scholarship. His plan was to go to New York and make money so he could go back to school. But once he got to Harlem, he didn't want to leave.

"To be young, gifted and black."

Think about those words, youngster — close your eyes and say them. They make a happy sound!

Lorraine Hansberry wrote those words. She was the youngest person, and the first African American, to win the New York Drama Critics Circle Award for a play. It's called *A Raisin in the Sun*, and it's the story of a black family and some of the struggles they go through trying to get themselves a good life.

Lorraine was born in Chicago in 1930. When she was a girl, her family moved to a white neighborhood. Once they got there, their neighbors tried to get rid of them. Lorraine's family had bricks thrown at them, and for a while, they lived with armed guards. Their neighbors got the Hansberrys to leave by saying there was a law that only white people could live in that neighborhood. But the Hansberrys would not sit still for that kind of prejudice. They took their fight against that law all the way to the Supreme Court of the United States. And you know what, youngster? They won!

Lorraine studied art in Chicago and theater at the University of Wisconsin. She moved to New York, got into politics, and got involved in the Civil Rights Movement. She wrote articles for *Freedom,* a newspaper started by Paul Robeson. Mr. Robeson was an actor and a great singer. She was also friends with James Baldwin, a writer you'll hear more about later.

Lorraine Hansberry

A Raisin in the Sun was produced in 1959. Lorraine's play was famous on Broadway. It was one of the first times that people had seen black characters who acted like real people, not like cartoons or stereotypes. *A Raisin in the Sun* was also a movie. Sadly, Lorraine died of cancer when she was just 34. After she died, her ex-husband published a book of her writings called *To Be Young, Gifted and Black.*

Prize. Her novel, *Maud Martha*, is based on her life. Gwendolyn took part in the Civil Rights Movement during the 1960s. She has been awarded more than 50 honorary degrees from colleges and universities.

These three writers and many others helped make it easier for a lot of other black writers. And their novels, plays, and poetry helped give a voice to the times ahead.

'TO BE YOUNG, GIFTED AND BLACK'

Have you heard of Gwendolyn Brooks, youngster? Well, she was the first African American author to win a Pulitzer Prize. She said once that when she writes, she reaches out to "black people in taverns, black people in alleys, black people in gutters, schools, offices, factories, prisons, ... black people in mines, on farms, on thrones."

Gwendolyn was the oldest child in her family. Her daddy was a janitor. She was born in 1917, and she grew up in Chicago. Gwendolyn loved words, and even when she was just a teenager, writers like Langston Hughes and James Weldon Johnson read her poems and told her to keep on writing.

Gwendolyn's writing is about ordinary people. Her first book of poetry, *A Street in Bronzeville*, was printed in 1945. Her second book, *Annie Allen*, was printed in 1949. That's the book that won the Pulitzer

Gwendolyn Brooks

Gwendolyn Brooks:

WE REAL COOL

The Pool Players.
Seven at the Golden Shovel.

We real cool. We
Left school. We

Lurk late. We
Strike straight. We

Sing sin. We
Thin gin. We

Jazz June. We
Die soon.

CHAPTER FOUR

BLACK A

Shush — do you hear that, child?

> "I have a dream
>
> that my four
>
> little children
>
> will one day live
>
> in a nation
>
> where they
>
> will not be judged
>
> by the color
>
> of their skin
>
> but by the content
>
> of their character."

That was the Reverend Dr. Martin Luther King, Jr., speaking. He sure knew how to talk to people, didn't he? He made that speech in front of a huge crowd gathered together in Washington, D.C., in 1963.

I remember it like it was yesterday.

Black folks had been fighting for their civil rights for a long time. In many parts of the United States, they couldn't vote, or hold certain jobs, or even be in the same places as white folks. But a few brave people were getting sick and tired of that situation and beginning to change it.

On the first of December in 1955, Mrs. Rosa Parks got on a crowded bus in Montgomery, Alabama. She found a seat near the rear of the bus, where she was expected to sit. Back then, black folks in the South were only allowed to sit in the back of the bus. Blacks were also expected to give up their seats to whites if the front of the bus was crowded. When a white man boarded the bus, Mrs. Parks was told to get up so the man could have her seat. She refused. She said she had paid the bus fare, she was tired, and she had a right to sit. She was arrested. When Mrs. Parks refused to give up her seat, everyone in the country found out about it.

That's because Dr. Martin Luther King, Jr., led folks in a protest after

Mrs. Parks's arrest. No black people would ride the buses in Montgomery. That bus company lost a lot of money. More important, some say it was the real beginning of the Civil Rights Movement.

Things had been heading toward a protest for a long time. For one thing, in 1954, the Supreme Court decided that it was illegal to keep whites and blacks in separate schools. Folks were talking more and more about how unfairly African Americans were treated. But when Mrs. Parks refused to give up her seat on that bus, well, that's when it all came together. I tell you, something really clicked that day. It was like a whole new world opened up.

Dr. King said African Americans should fight to get more freedom — but they should do it in a nonviolent way. He said black folks should be integrated into the rest of society. He meant they should have the same rights as white people, and live with them, side by side. With leaders like Dr. King, folks began thinking about what it really meant to love and respect themselves.

Malcolm X was another leader who talked about the love black people should have for themselves. But his way of doing things was different from Dr. King's. He was born Malcolm Little, but he later called himself Malcolm X because, he said, "Little" was the name that slave owners gave his family way back, not his true name. He said the X was for his lost African name.

Malcolm wrote a book with the writer Alex Haley called

Top to bottom on left: Malcolm X, singer James Brown, and a burning bus carrying Freedom Riders in the South. The Freedom Riders were people who worked against segregation and Jim Crow laws. Below right: Dr. Martin Luther King, Jr., addressing the huge crowd at the 1963 March on Washington

The Autobiography of Malcolm X, which came out in 1965. It told about his hard life and his ideas about how to make things better for blacks. Just like Dr. King, Malcolm knew a lot about what it meant to be treated unfairly because of his color. He was one of the smartest kids in his class at school, but when he told one of his teachers that he wanted to be a lawyer, the teacher just laughed at him. The teacher told Malcolm that he could never be a lawyer, because he was black. I guess the joke was on that teacher, though, because Malcolm grew up to be one of the most famous leaders of them all.

But before he did that, Malcolm fell on some hard times. He was a thief and a gambler for a time when he was young. He landed himself in prison for some of the things he did. When he was there, he joined the Black Muslims, or the Nation of Islam. For a while, he was their spokesman. Malcolm thought that black people should look out for themselves, and should fight if they were attacked by whites. He didn't think integration was the answer to the problems black folks faced. He thought that it was more important for black people to have the money to take care of themselves. Eventually, Malcolm changed some of his views. He decided that blacks and whites could work together. But he never stopped talking about black pride, or trying to help folks help themselves.

Above: Rosa Parks
Left: James Baldwin
Below: Amiri Baraka
Right: Nikki Giovanni

Dr. King and Malcolm X were both preachers. Their sermons and talks in front of large crowds stirred people up. There were many other black leaders who could get people thinking about their lives. Huey Newton and Bobby Seale and the Black Panthers said that black folks should stand up for themselves. James Brown encouraged people to sing "Say it loud, I'm black and I'm proud!" Folks wrote about brave hearts and the struggle for civil rights.

Sure enough, youngster, I was there.

So were James Baldwin, Nikki Giovanni, Paule Marshall, Amiri Baraka, Sonia Sanchez, Gordon Parks, and a whole lot of other folks.

James Arthur Baldwin was born in Harlem in 1924. He was the oldest of nine brothers and sisters. His stepfather was a preacher. James spent three years as a junior minister in his stepdaddy's church — starting when he was just 14 years old.

After his stepdaddy died in 1943, James moved to Greenwich Village, a New York neighborhood filled with artists and writers. That's where he met Richard Wright, who helped him win an award so he could keep on writing. After a few years, James left America because he felt that things were too hard for black folks here. He moved to France and spent most of his life there. But his writing was mostly about America. And he wrote all kinds of things. There was *Go Tell It on the Mountain,* which was based on his life growing up poor in Harlem. There was *Notes of a Native Son, The Fire Next Time, The Amen Corner,* and *Blues for Mister Charlie.* The last two were plays on Broadway. James worked for Dr. King and the Civil Rights Movement. And he wrote about how individual people could work to make their own lives better. His ideas weren't always popular. But he was a brave man, and he wrote what he thought. In those days, the writer to be like was James Baldwin. In this way, he lit a flame for many young people who wanted to be writers.

Another man who began writing just shortly after James Baldwin did is Amiri Baraka. He was born with the name Everett LeRoy Jones, but he changed it to LeRoi Jones when he went to college. Then he changed it again when his life changed. Amiri was born in Newark, New Jersey, in 1934. He was one of the only black students in his high school. He went to college for a few years, and then he joined the Air Force. When he left in 1957, he moved to New York and started publishing his writing in magazines and newspapers. Amiri hung out with lots of famous poets and writers of the time — people like Allen Ginsberg and Jack Kerouac. These poets and writers called themselves "Beats," and they wrote things that really bothered some people. Most of the Beats were white, and Amiri decided that they weren't doing enough talking about politics and the problems in America.

After the early 1960s, he stopped working with the Beats and began to write about racial issues.

Amiri is another writer who wears many hats. He is a poet and he's written plays. He's also written about music. His most famous play is *Dutchman.* It's about a meeting between a black man and a white woman on a subway car. After you read *Dutchman,* you realize that Amiri didn't hold out much hope that blacks and whites could get along.

Many people think Amiri's life is almost a guide to how blacks thought in the 1950s and '60s. His name changes, his ideas about black life, and his whole attitude make him very important in literature. He helped bring attention to the ideas within black culture and the black community.

Nikki Giovanni is another important writer from this time. Her work also focuses on the black community. Nikki was born in 1943 in Knoxville, Tennessee. Her given name is Yolande Cornelia Giovanni, Jr. She grew up in Ohio. She went to college and earned a degree in history from Fisk University.

Nikki is a poet — and a very good one. Many of her early poems are political. They're based on her work in the Civil Rights Movement. Her later work is more personal, and she wrote many poems about herself and her family. She's also written poems for children. She teaches college and continues to write. That's what writers do, child. They *have* to write. Just like the people we'll be meeting now.

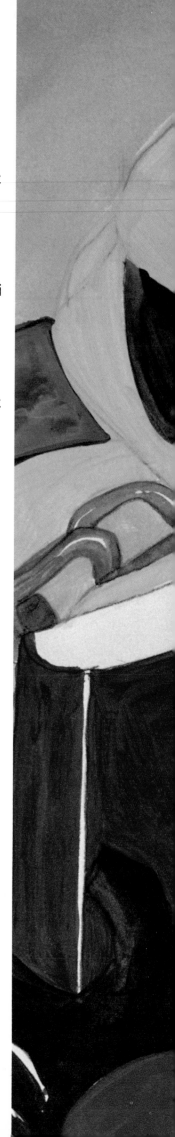

Nikki Giovanni:

*And though you're poor it isn't poverty that
concerns you
and though they fought a lot
it isn't your father's drinking that makes any difference
but only that everybody is together and you
and your sister have happy birthdays and very good
Christmases
and I really hope no white person ever has cause
to write about me
because they never understand
Black love is Black wealth and they'll
probably talk about my hard childhood
and never understand that
all the while I was quite happy*

from "Nikki-Rosa"

CHAPTER FIVE

REDISCOVERING OURSELVES

Alice Walker

Toni Morrison

Maya Angelou

hen Dr. King was killed in 1968, there were a lot of folks who thought the Civil Rights Movement was over.

But what he had started could not be easily undone. Dr. King dreamed that we were all beloved creatures under the sun, child. His dreams cushioned the dreams of folks like Alex Haley, Alice Walker, Maya Angelou, and Toni Morrison.

Alex was the man who helped Malcolm X write his story, and he dreamed of finding his kin in Africa. He did, and wrote a partly made-up account of his family's story in *Roots*. He traced his family tree all the way back to a man named Kunta Kinte, who was captured as a slave in Africa. It seems like everybody in the country read *Roots* or watched the television movie made from the book. It got folks interested in where they came from and who their people were. Some of the folks around here got fairly carried away with the prospect of finding long-lost relatives. I went looking for some of my own. I tickle myself sometimes just thinking about it.

I suppose lots of us found relatives hither and yon. My mama used to say, "You can never have too much family." I think she was right.

I'll tell you about three folks I'd like to meet, youngster — Alice Walker, Maya Angelou, and Toni Morrison. We're not related but I'd like to meet them.

Alice was born in Georgia in 1944. Her folks were sharecroppers. That means they rented land from an owner so they could farm. Many people call sharecropping just another form of slavery. Alice thought so. See, her folks always ended up owing the owner money at the end of the growing year, so they had to stay on that land and grow more crops to pay him off.

Alice felt strong ties to her family and the people in the small town where she grew up. When she was a little older, those folks got together and gave her a little bit of money so she could go away to school. Education for the young folks was real important to the people in that town. They didn't want their kids to be sharecroppers, too.

Alice got more money for school in a strange way. See, when she was eight years old, Alice's brother shot her in the eye with a BB gun. She's been blind in one eye ever since. Funny how some things that seem bad at first turn out to be good. Because of the accident, Alice got a scholarship that helped her go to college. If it hadn't been for her eye, she couldn't have afforded to go.

So Alice went away to school. She studied at Spelman College and at Sarah Lawrence College, and then she decided to become a writer. That feeling for family and community is in her writing. She admired Zora Neale Hurston. You remember her, don't you? Alice made people rediscover who Zora was and what she had written. One of Alice's best-known books is *The Color Purple*. It's about a woman named Celie who goes through a lot of hard times before she learns to love herself. They made a big movie out of that book. Alice has also written other novels, plus books of essays and lots of poetry.

Then there's Maya Angelou — gracious! — she can make words sing right from the pages they're written on. Maya had a tough life growing up. She was born Marguerite Johnson in St. Louis in 1928, and she spent most of her early years with her grandmama in Arkansas. When she was eight years old, her mother's boyfriend molested her, and then he turned up dead. Maya thought it was her fault. She got so scared, she didn't talk for years after that. Her mother took her to San Francisco, where she went to high school and became a dancer. That's when she changed her name to Maya Angelou. Later on, she moved to New York. It was there that Maya wrote *I Know Why the Caged Bird Sings*, the story of her early life. *The Heart of a Woman* and other books about her life came later. She wrote a lot of poetry, too. In fact, she wrote a poem for the 1993 presidential inauguration and recited it for the entire country. That poem is called "On the Pulse of Morning."

Looking at all she's done, I think Toni Morrison was always meant to be a writer. She was born Chloe Anthony Wofford in 1931 in the small town of Lorain, Ohio. Although she grew up in a family that didn't have a lot of money, her parents made sure she never felt less than anyone else.

Toni was one of only three black students in her first grade class, and she was the only student who knew how to read. Toni carried the strength from her family and love of books with her when she left her small town. She went to Howard University and she worked as a book editor for a while. Then she wrote a book called *The Bluest Eye*. It's about a young black girl who thinks her life would be a lot better if she only had blue eyes. This girl lives in a family where the people don't take care of each other. Toni tells about another family in the story that is strong and loving. She wrote lots of other books — *Sula* and *Beloved* and *Jazz* and *Song of Solomon* — but *The Bluest Eye* made me cry.

Toni's books have touched a lot of people, child.

She writes about community and family, and she says all of her stories start in that small town where she grew up, even if they don't take place there. In 1993, she became the first African American to win the Nobel Prize for Literature. That's the greatest award any writer can get. It means people think she's one of the best writers in the world. Think of that, youngster. Back in the days of slavery, people could be killed for learning to read and write. That didn't stop them. They risked their lives so great writers like Toni Morrison and Langston Hughes and Richard Wright and a lot of other fine novelists and poets and playwrights could bring their words out into the open.

I had to stop talking.

I discovered that to

achieve perfect personal

silence all I had to do was to

attach myself leechlike to sound. I

began to listen to everything. I probably

hoped that after I had heard all the sounds,

really heard them and packed them down,

deep in my ears, the world would be quiet

around me. I walked into rooms where people

were laughing, their voices hitting the walls

like stones, and I simply stood still — in the

midst of the riot of sound. After a minute or

two, silence would rush into the room from

its hiding place because I had eaten

up all the sounds.

from *I Know Why the Caged Bird Sings*

Lookit there, youngster — we've come back to the beginning. Winding up at this spot reminds me of a story. Not a once-upon-a-time story. A story about a teacher of mine.

I was learning to write my stories down, you see. And she came up to me as I sat wrestling with a pesky ending. I looked up at her and she must have seen trouble written all over my face.

Well, her lips began to curl up at the corners, her brow began to wrinkle. Next thing I knew, a big old smile popped out all over her face. She said, "Young man, every story has got to come full circle."

Well, child, I'm older now — you probably have noticed that my steps are a little slower.

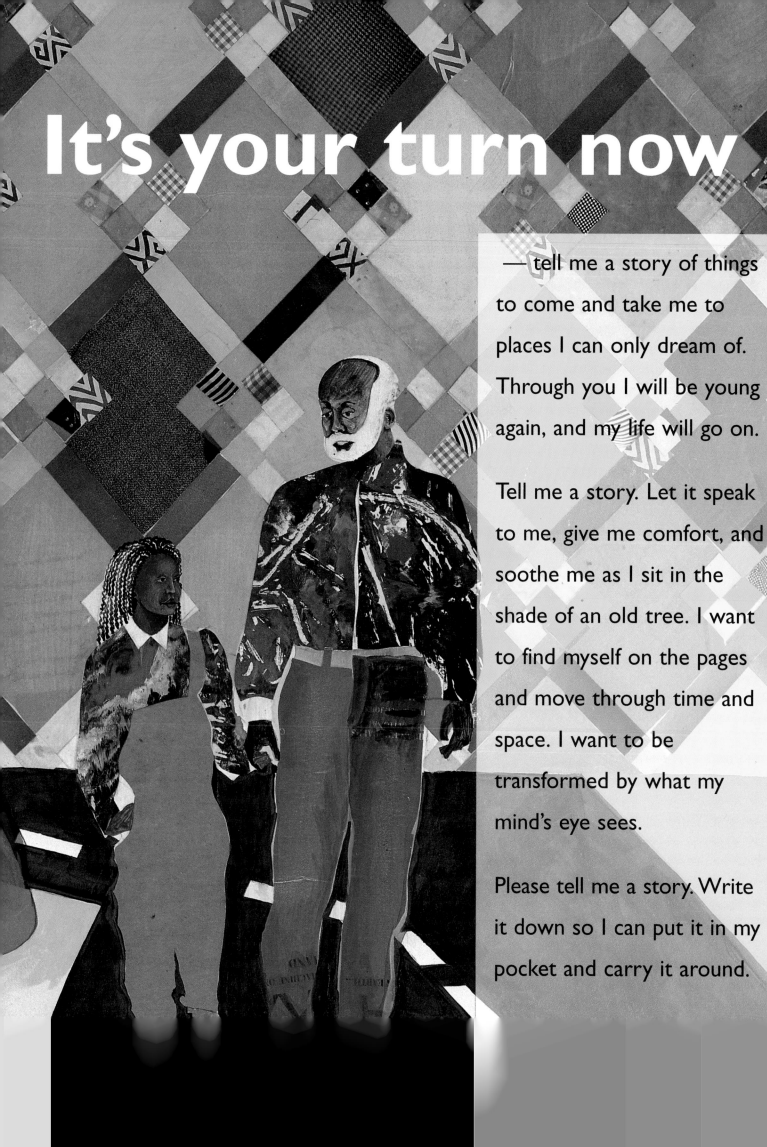

It's your turn now

—tell me a story of things to come and take me to places I can only dream of. Through you I will be young again, and my life will go on.

Tell me a story. Let it speak to me, give me comfort, and soothe me as I sit in the shade of an old tree. I want to find myself on the pages and move through time and space. I want to be transformed by what my mind's eye sees.

Please tell me a story. Write it down so I can put it in my pocket and carry it around.

GLOSSARY

CHAPTER 1
TO READ, TO WRITE — TO BE FREE

abolition — A movement that was dedicated to eliminating slavery.

Charles Chesnutt — The first African American to have a story published in a major national magazine. His books include *The Conjure Woman* and *The House Behind the Cedars*, published in 1899 and 1900.

Civil War — War fought between the northern and southern areas of the United States between 1861 and 1865. The North won and slavery was ended.

culture — All the customs and arts of a group of people, including language.

dialect — In this case, a style of writing that supposedly mimicked the speech patterns of African Americans.

generation — All the people born in the same time period.

Jim Crow laws — Set of laws enacted after the Civil War that kept African Americans separate from whites in nearly all areas of daily life, and kept them from voting and holding political office.

Ku Klux Klan — A group started after the Civil War by white southerners to terrorize black people. During some time periods, the Klan has been very powerful, and it has been responsible for the lynchings of many black people. It still exists today.

lynching — A mob of people terrorizing and killing another person, usually by hanging.

novel — A long fictional story printed in a book.

slave — Person who is owned and controlled by another.

slave narratives — Stories written by former slaves about their lives, the conditions they lived under, and how they got their freedom.

Supreme Court — The highest court in the United States.

CHAPTER 2
"WE" — A PEOPLE

anthem — A song of praise, devotion, or patriotism.

Communist Party — A political group or party whose main idea is that the government should own most of a nation's wealth and share it with the citizens.

Cotton Club — A popular white-owned nightclub in Harlem where many famous black musicians, singers, and dancers performed.

Countee Cullen — A major poet of the Harlem Renaissance, he was one of the first to write about the importance of African heritage to African Americans.

W.E.B. Du Bois — One of the founders of the National Association for the Advancement of Colored People (NAACP) and the author of *The Souls of Black Folk*, a collection of essays about race and politics.

Duke Ellington — Jazz musician and composer who first became famous during the 1920s in Harlem.

Marcus Garvey — Leader of a black nationalist movement that began in 1911 called the Universal Negro Improvement Association. Mr. Garvey believed that black Americans should live separately from white Americans, perhaps in their own country in Africa.

Harlem Renaissance — Period from about 1919 to 1929 when African American literature, art, and music flowered in Harlem, an area in New York City.

Claude McKay — Jamaican-born writer who was a major figure of the Harlem Renaissance. His works include the poetry collection *Harlem Shadows* and the novel *Home to Harlem.*

nationalism — A group of people's sense of belonging together as a nation. It includes pride in culture and heritage, and even a desire for national independence.

prejudice — An unfair opinion about a person or group based on external characteristics, feelings, and misinformation, not facts.

renaissance — In this case, a rebirth or flowering of literature, art, and music.

segregation — As used here, keeping people separate because of their skin color.

Mamie Smith — Singer who recorded a song called "Crazy Blues" in 1920. It is thought to be the first recording ever made of African American music.

symbol — Something that stands for something else; in this case, a place that stands for the hopes and dreams of a group of people.

Jean Toomer — Author of the novel *Cane*, about African American life and spirituality.

World War One — A war fought between 1914 and 1918 that involved many of the nations of the world. The United States fought in the war from 1917 to 1918.

CHAPTER 3
TO BE FREE ONCE MORE

classic — A creative work that is read, appreciated, and cherished for many years after it is published.

discriminate — In this case, to treat someone unfairly because of his or her race.

Great Depression — The period from 1929 to 1941 when millions of people were unemployed and many businesses shut down in the United States.

integration — The opposite of segregation — that is, the idea that all places should be open equally to all people regardless of their race.

A. Philip Randolph — Important labor and civil rights leader. He organized the Brotherhood of Sleeping Car Porters in 1925, the first African American labor union. He also helped organize the 1963 March on Washington, D.C.

Paul Robeson — Celebrated athlete, actor, and singer who worked for many African American causes, even though his career suffered because of it.

stereotype — A simplified exaggeration of something. Stereotypes are often used to put people down.

Tuskegee Airmen — Group of African American military pilots who trained together and then flew missions together in World War Two.

World War Two — A war fought between 1939 and 1945 that involved most of the nations in the world. The United States was in the war from 1941 to 1945.

CHAPTER 4
BLACK AND PROUD

autobiography — The story of a person's life, written by the person.

Black Panthers — Militant group that established inner-city programs and believed that blacks should defend themselves with violence.

James Brown — Popular African American singer during the 1960s who sang about black pride.

civil rights — In this case, all the rights guaranteed to the citizens of the United States. These rights include freedom of speech, religion, and the right to be treated equally and fairly by the government.

Civil Rights Movement — The movement to win full civil rights for African Americans has been going on for a long time. However, the modern movement began in the 1950s with court cases, boycotts, sit-ins, protest marches, and other actions.

essay — A short written piece that gives the writer's reasoned opinions on an issue or idea.

Dr. Martin Luther King, Jr. — Baptist minister who was a top leader of the Civil Rights Movement. Dr. King preached nonviolence in his efforts to gain full civil rights for African Americans. He won the Nobel Peace Prize in 1964 after the spectacular success of the March on Washington. At this march, Dr. King delivered his famous "I Have a Dream" speech.

Paule Marshall — A novelist and short story writer, her books include *Brown Girl, Brownstones* and *Praisesong for the Widow*.

Huey Newton — Co-founder, with Bobby Seale, of the Black Panthers.

Gordon Parks — A photographer and movie director, he has also written many books, including *The Learning Tree*.

Sonia Sanchez — A poet and playwright, her books include *We a BaddDDD People, homegirls & handgrenades,* and *It's a New Day*.

CHAPTER 5
REDISCOVERING OURSELVES

sharecropper — Farmer who pays a landowner rent with part of the crops grown during the year.

SELECTED READING MATERIAL

This is a selected list of the works of the writers mentioned in this book. Some of these works may not be suitable for younger children.

Maya Angelou: *I Know Why the Caged Bird Sings*, autobiography, 1970; *Just Give Me a Cool Drink of Water 'fore I Diiie*, poetry, 1971; *Gather Together in My Name*, autobiography, 1974; *And Still I Rise*, poetry, 1978; *I Shall Not Be Moved*, poetry, 1990.

James Baldwin: *Go Tell It on the Mountain*, novel, 1953; *The Amen Corner*, play, 1955; *Notes of a Native Son*, essays, 1961; *The Fire Next Time*, essays, 1963; *Blues for Mister Charlie*, play, 1964; *Another Country*, novel, 1965.

Amiri Baraka: *Preface to a Twenty Volume Suicide Note*, poetry, 1961; *Dutchman*, play, 1964; *The System of Dante's Hell*, novel, 1965; *The Autobiography of LeRoi Jones*, autobiography, 1984; *The Music: Reflections on Jazz and Blues*, history, 1987.

Gwendolyn Brooks: *A Street in Bronzeville*, poetry, 1945; *Annie Allen*, poetry, 1949; *Maud Martha*, novel, 1953; *The Bean Eaters*, poetry, 1960; *City*, poetry, 1983.

William Wells Brown: *Narrative of William W. Brown, a Fugitive Slave, Written by Himself*, slave narrative, 1847; *Clotel: Or, The President's Daughter*, novel, 1853.

Charles W. Chesnutt: *The Conjure Woman*, short stories, 1899; *The Wife of His Youth, and Other Stories of the Color Line*, short stories, 1899; *The House Behind the Cedars*, novel, 1900.

Countee Cullen: *Color*, poetry, 1925; *Copper Sun*, poetry, 1927; *One Way to Heaven*, novel, 1932.

Frederick Douglass: *Narrative of the Life of Frederick Douglass, an American Slave, Written by Himself*, slave narrative, 1845; *The Heroic Slave*, short novel, 1855; *The Life and Times of Frederick Douglass*, speeches and articles, 1881.

W.E.B. Du Bois: *The Souls of Black Folk*, essays, 1903.

Paul Laurence Dunbar: *Majors and Minors*, poetry, 1895; *Lyrics of Lowly Life*, poetry, 1896; *The Sport of the Gods*, novel, 1902.

Ralph Ellison: *Invisible Man*, novel, 1952; *Shadow and Act*, essays, 1964; *Going to the Territory*, essays, 1986.

Olaudah Equiano: *The Interesting Narrative of the Life of Olaudah Equiano, or Gustavus Vassa, the African, Written by Himself*, slave narrative, 1789.

Nikki Giovanni: *Black Feeling, Black Talk*, poetry, 1967; *Black Judgement*, poetry, 1968; *Spin a Soft Black Song*, children's poetry, 1972; *My House*, poetry, 1972; *Ego-Tripping and Other Poems for Young People*, children's poetry, 1973; *Shimmy Shimmy Shimmy Like My Sister Kate: Looking at the Harlem Renaissance through Poems* (editor), poetry, 1996; *The Sun Is So Quiet*, children's poetry, 1996.

Alex Haley: *The Autobiography of Malcolm X*, co-written with Malcolm X, autobiography, 1965; *Roots*, novel, 1976.

Lorraine Hansberry: *A Raisin in the Sun*, play, 1959; *To Be Young, Gifted and Black: Lorraine Hansberry in Her Own Words*, collected writings, 1969.

Langston Hughes: *The Weary Blues*, poetry, 1926; *Not Without Laughter*, novel, 1930; *The Dream Keeper and Other Poems*, poetry, 1932; *Simple Speaks His Mind*, short stories, 1950; *Ask Your Mama: 12 Moods for Jazz*, poetry, 1961; *Simple's Uncle Sam*, short stories, 1965; *The Panther and the Lash*, poetry, 1967.

Zora Neale Hurston: *Mules and Men*, folktales, 1934; *Their Eyes Were Watching God*, novel, 1937; *Tell My Horse*, folktales, 1938; *Dust Tracks on a Road*, autobiography, 1942.

James Weldon Johnson: *The Autobiography of an Ex-Colored Man*, novel, 1912; *The Book of American Negro Poetry* (editor), poetry, 1922; *God's Trombone: Seven Negro Sermons in Verse*, poetry, 1927.

Martin Luther King, Jr.: *Stride Toward Freedom: The Montgomery Story*, history, 1958; *Letter from Birmingham City Jail*, essay, 1963; *The Trumpet of Conscience*, essays, 1968.

Malcolm X: *The Autobiography of Malcolm X*, co-written with Alex Haley, autobiography, 1965; *Malcolm X Speaks*, speeches, 1965.

Paule Marshall: *Brown Girl, Brownstones*, novel, 1949; *Soul Clap Hands and Sing*, short stories, 1961; *Praisesong for the Widow*, novel, 1983.

Claude McKay: *Harlem Shadows*, poetry, 1922; *Home to Harlem*, novel, 1928; *A Long Way from Home*, autobiography, 1937.

Toni Morrison: *The Bluest Eye*, novel, 1969; *Sula*, novel, 1973; *Song of Solomon*, novel, 1977; *Beloved*, novel, 1987; *Jazz*, novel, 1992.

Gordon Parks: *The Learning Tree*, novel, 1963; *Born Black*, essays, 1971; *Voices in the Mirror*, autobiography, 1990.

Paul Robeson: *Here I Stand*, autobiography, 1958.

Sonia Sanchez: *Homecoming*, poetry, 1969; *We a BaddDDD People*, poetry, 1970; *homegirls and handgrenades*, poetry, 1984; *Wounded in the House of a Friend*, poetry, 1995.

Jean Toomer: *Cane*, novel, 1923; *Balo*, play, 1927.

Alice Walker: *The Third Life of Grange Copeland*, novel, 1970; *Revolutionary Petunias and Other Poems*, poetry, 1970; *Meridian*, novel, 1976; *The Color Purple*, novel, 1982; *The Temple of My Familiar*, novel, 1989.

Phillis Wheatley: *Poems on Various Subjects, Religious and Moral*, poetry, 1773.

Richard Wright: *Uncle Tom's Children*, four short stories, 1938; *Native Son*, novel, 1940; *Black Boy: A Record of Childhood and Youth*, autobiography, 1945.